TREE

Written by Olivia Watson

Illustrated by Tjarda Borsboom

First published in 2024 by Hungry Tomato Ltd.
F15, Old Bakery Studios, Blewetts Wharf,
Malpas Road, Truro, Cornwall, TR1 1QH, UK.

Thanks to our creative team:
Editor: Holly Thornton
Editor: Millie Burdett
Senior Designer: Amy Harvey

ISBN: 9781916598621

Printed and bound in China

Discover more at
www.hungrytomato.com
www.mybeetlebooks.com

Contents

What Is a Tree? — 8

What Do Trees Need? — 10

How Do Trees Grow? — 12

The Water Cycle — 14

Spreading Seeds — 16

Types of Trees — 18

Tree Protection — 20

Tree Adaptations — 22

Friendly Forests — 24

Mysterious Rainforest — 26

Layers of a Rainforest — 28

Surviving in the Swamp — 30

Life in the Desert — 32

Family Trees — 34

Nature's Compass — 36

Tree Awards — 38

Young or Old? 40

Stunning Looks 42

Smelliest Trees 44

Trees and Me 46

Good and Bad 48

Animal Homes 50

Wildlife Homes 52

Healthy Planet 54

Let's Plant a Tree 56

Did You Know? 58

Glossary 60

Index 61

Words in **BOLD** can be found in the glossary.

What Is a Tree?

Trees are living things that can be found almost everywhere on Earth! They are important for people and nature. Trees come in all shapes and sizes, but most have the same four parts.

Branches

A tree's branches grow outward from its trunk. It's here that leaves, fruit, flowers and nuts grow.

Crown

Leaves

Leaves are very important. They help the tree make its own food to give it energy and help it grow.

Trunk

The trunk acts as a drinking straw, carrying water and **nutrients** from the roots to different parts of the tree.

Roots

Roots are usually hidden underground. They help to hold the tree in place, like an anchor.

Twig

Fruit

Some trees have other features, such as fruit, which are full of hidden seeds.

Not a tree

Some plants that we call trees aren't trees at all! Cacti and boojum aren't made of wood, and palms don't have branches, so they don't count!

Cactus

Boojum tree

Palm tree

What Do Trees Need?

Trees can't grow without a few very important things: sunlight, air, water, and nutrients.

Sun

Trees take light from the Sun and turn it into food, which gives them energy to grow.

Water

Without enough water, trees would shrivel up and die.

Air

Just like us, trees need plenty of air to stay alive. They use it to make food!

Nutrients

A tree's roots take up nutrients and water from the soil that it needs to grow.

Insects

Bugs like bees and butterflies **pollinate** flowers, which helps trees grow fruit and seeds.

Space

Trees need lots of space around them to avoid **competing** with other trees for nutrients and sunlight.

Wildlife

Wildlife and trees help each other. Animals help trees spread their seeds, while branches and trunks make great woody homes.

How Do Trees Grow?

Every tree starts its life as a tiny seed, even the most gigantic ones! How does it all begin?

Seeds

Seeds come in all shapes and sizes, but they're all packed with food to keep the **seedling** alive until it grows and can make its own.

1.

Once planted and given water, a root starts to grow out from the seed. This is called **germination**.

2.

A shoot grows up from the seed toward the soil's surface as the root grows down.

3.

The roots keep growing as the shoot becomes a trunk. A young tree is called a sapling.

4.

The tree grows bigger and stronger, and starts growing flowers and fruit on its branches.

5.

Eventually, the tree gets weaker and stops growing. Even **decaying** trees make great homes for wildlife.

The Water Cycle

Trees need water to stay healthy and strong, but they also help water to be recycled across the world. We call this the water cycle.

2. Leaves

Even rainwater sat on leaves is swept up. Trees release extra water through their leaves if they have too much, too!

1. Evaporation

The Sun warms water from oceans and rivers, turning it into tiny droplets that rise into the air.

3. Condensation
Up in the sky, the water droplets cool down and stick together as clouds.

4. Precipitation
When clouds get very heavy, the water droplets fall back down as rain, snow, or hail.

5. Collection
Plants and rivers collect water that runs into the soil or ocean, then the cycle starts again!

Spreading Seeds

Trees can't move around like animals, so they have to find clever ways to spread their seeds.

Up, up and away

Some seeds are swept up and scattered by the wind. Winged seeds can fly far!

Willow tree

Birch tree

Water surfers

Some trees, like willows, lean over streams and rivers. Their seeds fall into the water and are carried away by the **current**.

Seedy surprise

Some animals eat the fruit from trees. They poop out the seeds they can't **digest**, leaving them to grow into new trees.

16

Exploding seeds

Some trees have **seedpods** that explode! Bursting open, they shoot their seeds as far away as they can.

Sticky seeds

Seeds with tiny spikes or hooks stick to animals' feathers or fur. They can be carried a long way before falling off.

Hidden treasure

Squirrels bury nuts and seeds, saving them for winter. The ones they forget about grow into trees!

Sandbox tree

Types of Trees

There are more than 60,000 types of trees in the world! They all fit into a main group based on how they grow: deciduous or evergreen.

Deciduous

Deciduous trees lose their leaves in fall/autumn and regrow them in spring.

Broadleaf

Most deciduous trees have wide, flat leaves.

Magnolia tree

Ash tree

Flowers and fruit

Only deciduous trees grow flowers! They can be all shapes and sizes, but only bloom for a short time every year.

Hardwood

Hardwood is another name for deciduous trees. They usually have heavy trunks and grow much slower than softwoods.

Evergreen

Evergreen trees don't lose their leaves in winter; they stay green all year round! Many evergreens are coniferous trees.

Needles

Scales

Coniferous

Coniferous trees have narrow, hard leaves called needles or scales.

Pine tree

White cedar tree

Cones

Conifers don't grow flowers; they make cones. These hard shells keep the seeds safe until they're ready to grow into new trees!

Softwood

This is another name for coniferous trees. They usually have lighter trunks, but aren't all soft: yew is harder than some hardwoods!

Tree Protection

Trees have clever ways of protecting themselves from the animals that try to hurt them, but sometimes they need a helping hand.

Acacia alert

When acacias are being eaten, they send out a warning! Nearby acacias release bitter **tannins** into their leaves to stop them being eaten next!

Helpful elephants

These gentle giants love to munch on young trees. This stops too many trees from competing for nutrients and space, meaning older trees can keep growing taller.

Undercover chemicals

Trees like oak and spruce also release tannins to make insects who eat them ill. What a nasty surprise!

Sap trap

Some trees, like lodgepole pines, release sticky **sap** that traps bugs, stopping them from eating the **bark** and killing the tree.

Food chain

The food chain keeps nature balanced; it stops **herbivores** from eating too many plants and trees.

Tree Adaptations

Trees live almost everywhere, from snowy mountains to dry deserts. They've found clever ways of **adapting** to these different places.

Leaves

Broadleaf leaves are wide to catch lots of sunlight in summer. Conifer needles are thin to stop snow smothering them in winter.

Growing tall

Trees in crowded, shady forests have to grow taller and taller to reach the sunlight that they need to survive!

Spring

Deciduous trees change through the seasons. In spring, new leaves grow and fruit trees **blossom**.

Summer

By summer, the branches are covered with thick green leaves, and fruit will soon start to grow.

Water adapting

The baobab can hold lots of water in its thick trunk, which helps it survive in the desert.

Fireproof

Trees in fire-prone areas, like the Ponderosa pine, grow extra thick bark to protect the trunk and help the tree survive fire.

Secret stash

The shortleaf pine hides **dormant** buds underground. If it's burnt down, it can regrow itself from these buds!

Fall/Autumn

In fall/autumn, leaves change from green to red, yellow, orange, or brown, and fall to the ground.

Winter

By winter, the branches are bare: the tree saves its energy, sleeping through the coldest months.

Friendly Forests

Forests are large areas of land that are covered in trees. Lots of different types of wildlife make their homes in forests.

Lively wildlife

Many animals make their homes in trees, while flowers and **fungi** grow all around. Forests are full of life!

Chestnut tree

Hickory tree

The shiny seeds from chestnut trees are hidden inside spiky little cases. This stops them from being eaten by hungry animals!

These trees grow egg-shaped nuts and flowers with no petals! Hickory trees have a deep **taproot** which makes them stand strong.

Silver birch tree

Beech tree

These trees have thin bark that peels off as they get older. Their flowers grow as **catkins**, which some people call "lambs' tails" because they look similar!

Beech trees can live for around 400 years! They grow huge dome-shaped crowns where insects and nesting birds love to shelter.

Mysterious Rainforest

Tropical rainforests are thick, lively forests that grow in hot, rainy places! They are home to thousands of different plants and animals.

Exciting discoveries

About half of all known plants live in the rainforest, but scientists think there are thousands more to discover!

Tasty treats

Lots of yummy things come from rainforest trees, like bananas and grapefruit!

Brazil nut tree

Famous for their tasty nuts, these giant trees tower over the rainforest and can live to be 1,000 years old!

Kapok tree

Some of the tallest around, Kapok grow up to 13 feet (4 m) a year. That's higher than a basketball hoop!

Strangler fig tree

Spooky strangler figs grow on top of other tree trunks. Winding their roots around, they completely take over!

Kauri tree

Look out below! These chunky-trunked trees drop their lower branches as they grow taller and taller.

Cecropia tree

These fast-growing trees shoot up in clearings, filling the space with their umbrella-like leaves.

Rubber tree

The thick, white sap from rubber trees is used to make everyday items like shoes, gloves and balls!

27

Layers of a Rainforest

Tropical rainforests are made up of different layers, with different plants and animals living in each part.

Emergent layer

Only the tallest trees reach the emergent layer. Up above the canopy, they get lots of sunlight, without needing to fight for it!

Canopy layer

The canopy is filled with trees reaching for sunlight. It blocks out light below! Many animals make their homes in the treetops.

Understory (understorey) layer

Damp and dark, only small trees and plants grow here. Animals can easily sneak around trees to catch their prey unaware!

Forest floor

Lots of insects live here. They eat fallen leaves and fruit, recycling nutrients in the soil and keeping it rich for trees to grow.

Surviving in the Swamp

Swamps are a special type of wetland; they're areas of land that are mostly filled with water, but lots of trees grow there.

What's that water?

Freshwater swamps form near lakes after heavy rain. Lots of animals live in and around swamp trees.

Rising roots

Swamp trees' roots grow near the surface of the soil to help them breathe in the water-logged soil.

Mighty Mangroves

These swamps fill with seawater during high tides! Salty water kills most plants, but not mangrove trees! Strong roots keep them standing and provide shelter for fish laying eggs.

Bald cypress

These trees have knees! Scientists think they help air reach the roots and keep trees standing.

Red maple

These fast-growing trees make thousands of seeds. Safe inside a winged case, they fly far on the wind.

White cedar

The Northern white cedar grows slowly in swamps, but can live for hundreds, maybe thousands, of years!

Life in the Desert

Deserts are dry places that get very little rain. Desert trees have clever ways of finding and storing water, which helps them survive in this harsh place.

Reaching roots

Some desert trees grow shallow, wide roots to catch as much rain as possible. Others grow long roots to reach water deep underground.

Waxy leaves

Lots of desert plants have small leaves covered in wax. Some don't have leaves; they have spikes! Both adaptations help reduce water loss.

Desert willow

Elephant tree

With bright flowers, this tree stands out in the desert, attracting pollinating insects like bees and hummingbirds!

This tree's name comes from its chunky trunk, which looks like an elephant's leg! It's perfect for storing lots of water.

Desert ironwood

Mesquite tree

This tree is in the same family as peas! It blooms in spring, providing shelter and nutrients for small plants and animals.

With some of the longest roots in the desert, mesquite trees are able to reach water hidden deep underground.

Tree-like disguises

Not everything with "tree" in its name is a tree! With branches and leaves, these sneaky plants trick people into thinking they're trees, but they are actually **succulents**, like cacti!

Joshua tree

Boojum tree

Family Trees

Trees often work together to help each other survive. Sometimes they even work with other living things!

Oak tree

Friendly fungi?

Some mushrooms hurt trees by making them sick! Others help them by sharing nutrients back and forth.

Wood wide web

Scientists think that fungi help trees talk to each other by joining their roots together. They call this the "wood wide web"!

Insect army

Sometimes nature teams up! Ants become bodyguards for acacia trees, defending them from hungry animals in exchange for food and shelter.

Family roots

Trees of the same family look out for each other, sharing nutrients with the young, old or sick. Some even help trees that are different from themselves, like fir and birch!

Beech tree

Chemical protection

Not all trees get along. Beech trees release chemicals from their roots to keep others away. This gives young beech trees more space to grow.

Nature's Compass

The way trees grow can be affected by the weather! The direction of the wind and sunshine can make a big difference to how they look.

Sunlight slant

Like most plants, trees grow toward the Sun. In the Northern **hemisphere**, trees grow toward the South; in the Southern hemisphere, they grow toward the North.

Seeking shelter

Mosses love to grow in damp, shady places. You'll often spot them growing on the sheltered side of tree trunks.

Fast fruit

Fruit that gets more time in the sun will ripen and be ready to eat before fruit that's in a shady spot.

Wild winds

Trees hit by wind don't grow as big, leaving rows of trees growing to different heights! This shape is called the "wedge effect".

Happy heart

They don't beat like ours, but trees have hearts too! This strong, dark wood runs up the trunk, supporting the tree.

Prevailing wind

In most places, the wind blows from one direction more than others. This is called a "prevailing wind", and it affects how trees grow.

Super strength

To cope with strong winds, some trees thicken parts of their trunk and roots to stop themselves being blown down.

Tree Awards

These record-breaking trees are some of the most impressive!

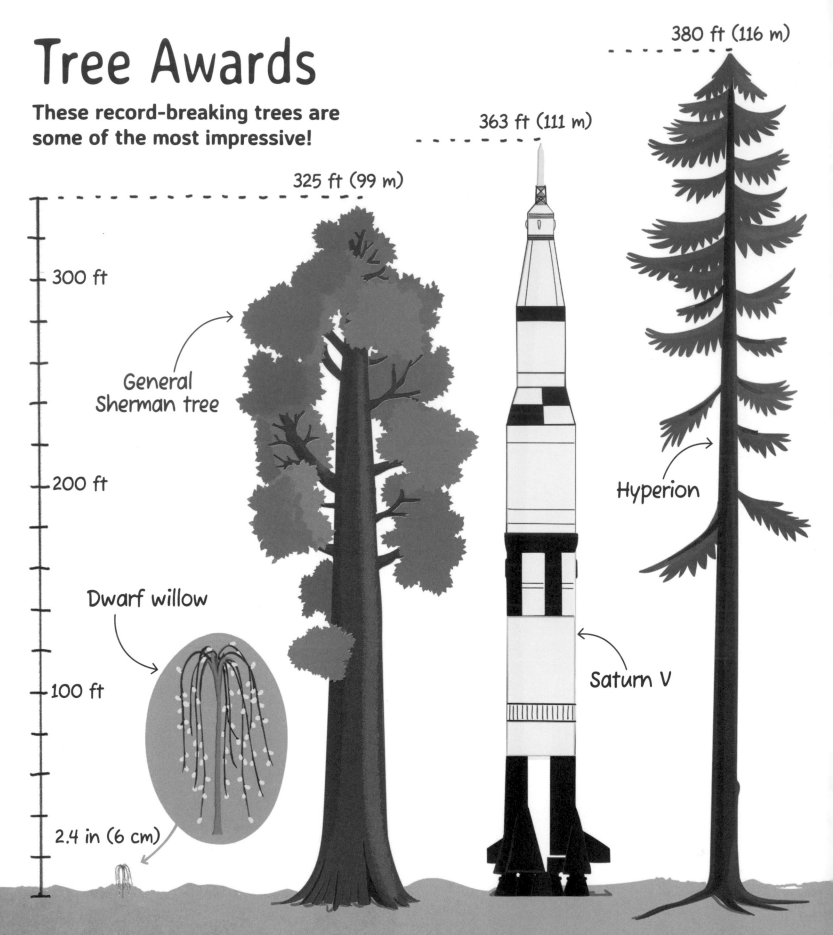

380 ft (116 m)

363 ft (111 m)

325 ft (99 m)

300 ft

General Sherman tree

200 ft

Dwarf willow

Hyperion

100 ft

Saturn V

2.4 in (6 cm)

Smallest tree
The dwarf willow is the smallest tree, growing to only 2.4 inches (6 cm) tall!

Largest tree
The General Sherman in California, USA, is the largest tree in the world!

Tallest tree
The Hyperion redwood tree is even taller than one of the tallest rockets: Saturn V.

El Árbol del Tule

Great Basin bristlecone tree

Widest tree

At a whopping 46 feet (14 m),
El Árbol del Tule in Mexico is the
widest tree in the world!

Oldest tree

The Great Basin bristlecone pine,
Methuselah, that's growing in the
USA is almost 5,000 years old!

Young or Old?

Trees are some of the oldest living things on our planet. They can't live forever, but even at the end of their lives, they're interesting plants!

Bell bottom

Old trees stop growing up, but keep growing out, giving them bell-shaped trunks. Dying trees that stay standing are called snags.

Nutrient delivery

Dead trees release nutrients into the soil, making it better for new plants and trees to grow.

Life after death

Even dead trees keep forests alive! Hollow logs make great animal homes, and rotting wood is yummy food for some fungi.

- - - - - - - - - 7 years

- - - - - - - - 6 years

- - - - - - - 5 years

Scientists have clever ways of working out how old trees are.

Age levels

Most conifers grow a circle of branches every year. We can count the groups to get a rough age. This works best for trees up to 20 years old.

- - - - - - - ← 4 years

- - - - - 3 years

- - - - - 2 years

Trunk rings

Every year, many trees grow another ring of wood inside their trunks. We can count the rings to figure out their age.

- - - - - 1 year

Stunning Looks

There are so many amazing-looking trees around the world. Which one do you think stands out the most?

Crooked Forest

These curved trees in Poland are surrounded by straight trees! No one knows why some are this strange shape.

Bonsai tree

These tiny trees can be trained to grow into beautiful shapes. The art of shaping bonsai is more than 1,000 years old.

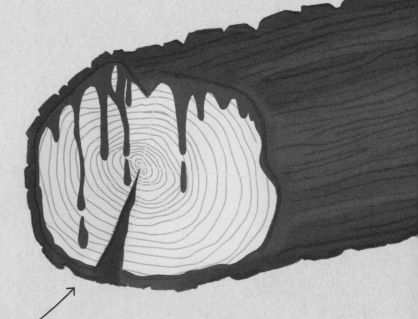

Dragon blood tree

This spooky tree is named for its thick red sap, which people once believed was the blood of dragons!

Silk cotton tree temples

Giant silk cotton trees have taken over an abandoned temple in Cambodia, twisting their roots around the stones.

Prison tree

This **sacred** boab tree in Australia, with its wide, hollow trunk, is claimed to have once been used to hold prisoners!

Topiary trees

From twirls to animal shapes, topiary is the art of creating living masterpieces out of trees!

Cannonball tree

Look out! This tree has big, heavy cannonball-like fruits that fall to the ground when ripe.

Smelliest Trees

Some plants smell good enough to eat,
while others might put you off your food!

Banana shrub

These pretty yellow flowers
smell just like bananas!

Caramel tree

These leaves smell like
caramel and toffee.

Some trees' smells come from
their flowers, and some come
from their leaves!

Yellowtail

These bright clusters of
flowers smell like pineapple.
Yum yum!

Callery pear

Don't get tricked by these pretty blossoms – they smell like rotting fish. Ew!

Ginkgo

This tree stinks! Most people think it smells like dirty gym socks or dog poop.

Kapok

This tree's flowers may smell horrible to us, but bats love them!

White spruce

When broken, these needles smell like a stinky skunk!

45

Trees and Me

Your home is probably filled with things that are made from trees.

Books
Paper is made from wood. Without trees, we wouldn't have books!

Toys
Toys, like train sets and dollhouses, are often made from wood.

Maple tree

Syrup
Lots of tasty things come from trees, like maple syrup, which is sap!

Furniture

Wood is made into lots of useful things for the house, including furniture like tables and chairs.

Cherry tree

Food

Many trees produce yummy fruits, like cherries, apples, or oranges, that people and animals like to eat.

Good and Bad

Some trees have healing powers and have been used in medicines for centuries, but others are deadly!

Alder tree

The bark from this tree can be turned into a medicinal tea that helps soothe sore throats.

alder tea

Manchineel

Also called "death apple tree"! The leaves give a nasty burn, and eating the fruit can be deadly.

Apple tree

Eating fruit helps keep us healthy. Apples are good for our stomachs and hearts, and they help us to avoid illness.

Elder tree

Lots of parts of the elder tree can be used in medicines, like the flowers, which help treat fevers, colds, and flu.

Spindle tree

With bright fruit and seeds, the spindle tree may look pretty, but it's **poisonous** to humans and many animals!

Strychnine

This tree contains a powerful poison. Once used in medicine in tiny amounts, it's now considered too dangerous and isn't allowed in lots of countries!

Willow bark

Willow tree bark has been used as a natural painkiller for more than 3,500 years!

Animal Homes

Lots of different animals around the world make their homes in and around trees.

Branch adventurers

Monkeys live in the treetops, using their strong arms or tails to swing from branch to branch in search of food.

Dam builders

Using strong teeth, beavers chew through tree trunks for wood to build their dams and special shelters called "lodges".

Leafy living

Some animals, like sloths, live in trees, using the leaves to hide from the bigger animals that hunt them.

Safety nest

Many birds build nests high in the trees to keep their babies away from animals that would try to eat them!

Hollow hideaways

Small animals live inside tree hollows where they're hidden and safe.

Beaver lodge

51

Wildlife Homes

Even the smallest creatures use trees for food and shelter, from up in the top branches to down on the ground.

Insect central

From butterflies eating **nectar** to beetles burrowing into fallen logs, trees are home to many insects.

Shady plants

It's not just animals; lots of plants can be found around trees, making the most of the shelter they provide.

Sneaky reptiles

Some crafty snakes and lizards are good at blending in with trees and can sneak up and catch other animals!

Let's Make a Wildlife Log House
Create a home for insects using nature finds!

You will need:

- Big pieces of wood
- Big logs
- Twigs
- Moss
- Leaves
- Cones

Important information:

When collecting natural materials, always ask permission and only take things that have fallen to the ground; don't break branches off trees or damage plants!

1. Adventure into a nearby woods to collect pieces of wood and logs. Always go with an adult to stay safe.

2. In your yard/garden, place two logs upright, leaving space in between. Ask an adult to secure them into the ground.

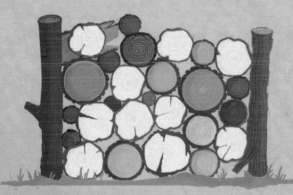

3. Pile the rest of the logs and wood as shown. You may need to collect more if they don't fill the space!

4. Collect smaller natural materials such as moss, twigs, leaves, and cones. Insects love all of these!

5. Use these to fill in any gaps and finish the log house. Check back daily to see which insects you can spot!

53

Healthy Planet

Trees play an important part in keeping our planet happy and healthy. We have a lot to thank them for!

Clean air

Trees use their leaves to turn **carbon dioxide** from the air into **oxygen**, which humans and animals need to breathe.

CO_2

Rich soil

Trees use their roots to bring nutrients from deep underground up to the surface, keeping soil healthy.

Pollution preventer

Tree roots act like sponges. They help to keep water clean by soaking up the things that could **pollute** it.

O^2

Global warming

Too much carbon dioxide can lead to **global warming**! Planting more trees will help to stop that from happening.

Happy habitats

Woods provide a great place for us to go and study nature, play, and have fun!

Let's Plant a Tree

Help the planet by planting your very own tree! Choosing the perfect planting place will help your tree to grow.

You will need:

- Tree sapling
- Shovel
- Watering can
- Stake/cane (to hold the tree upright)
- String

Where to plant

Some places have rules on planting trees, and some trees grow to be gigantic, so make sure an adult checks that your chosen spot is okay.

Choosing your tree

Choose a tree that's **native** to your area. It will be used to the weather and soil, and find it easier to grow!

Time to plant!

Tree planting seasons vary around the world – ask your local plant nursery for the best time to buy and plant your sapling.

1.

Ask an adult to cut the grass and pull up any weeds in the area you'll be planting your tree.

2.

Dig a hole deep enough for all the roots to fit in and twice as wide. Keep the soil close – you'll need it again soon.

3.

It's important that the sapling goes into a level hole, otherwise it won't grow properly!

4.

Place your sapling in the hole, making sure it fits inside comfortably and is standing up straight.

5.

Using the dug soil, refill the hole, making sure to cover all the roots. Press down around the trunk so that it's secure in the ground.

6.

Push your stake/cane 2 feet (60 cm) into the soil. Tie the sapling to it with string. This will help it stay upright, even in windy weather.

7.

Water the soil around your sapling to make it moist. It shouldn't need watering much after this; its roots will find water in the soil themselves.

8.

Trees grow at different speeds: some take 2-10 years and others take more than 30 to reach full size! Keep the area free from weeds and pests to help your tree grow. After 2-3 years, most trees should stand without the stake/cane.

Did You Know?

Trees are pretty amazing! Every living creature needs trees to survive, from eating them to living in them. The world wouldn't be the way it is today if we didn't have them. Did you know these amazing facts about trees?

It takes a raindrop
10 MINUTES
to reach the rainforest floor.

A large oak tree can drop as many as
10,000 ACORNS
in one year!

Trees have been on Earth for more than
350 MILLION YEARS!
That's way before dinosaurs walked the Earth!

Some trees have been to the **MOON!**
They were grown from seeds onboard
the Apollo 14 mission in 1971...

A quarter of the ingredients in
modern medicines come from

RAINFOREST PLANTS!

RAINFOREST REMEDIES

MEDICINES

Every year, people from all over the
world travel to Japan for Hanami, the
ancient tradition of enjoying the

BLOOMING OF CHERRY BLOSSOMS.

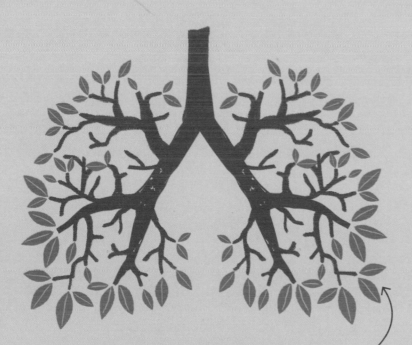

Trees are sometimes called the
"LUNGS OF THE EARTH"
because they filter the air to make it
clean for animals and humans to breathe.

Glossary

Adapting – (verb) when a living thing can survive in its surroundings by developing special features or skills over a long period of time.

Bark – the tough outer layer of a woody plant stem or root, such as a tree trunk.

Blossom - (verb) the process of fruit trees growing lots of flowers.

Carbon dioxide – an invisible gas in the air that plants take in to make food and oxygen.

Catkins - long, slim clusters of flowers that some trees grow to hold their seeds.

Competing – (verb) going against one another to gain or win something.

Current – the continuous movement of a body of water, such as a river or ocean.

Decaying – (verb) slowly breaking down over time. This happens to plants and animals after they've died.

Digest – (verb) to break down food into substances that can be absorbed and used by a body or plant.

Dormant – living things that are alive but not currently growing – it's like they're sleeping.

Fungi – (the plural of fungus). A group of living things, including mushrooms, molds/moulds, and yeasts, that are neither plants nor animals.

Germination – the process when a seed begins to sprout roots and shoots.

Global warming – the rising temperature of the planet, which causes climate change.

Habitat – the natural home of plants and animals.

Hemisphere – half of the Earth, divided by an invisible line through the middle. The countries in the top half are Northern and the ones in the bottom half are Southern.

Herbivores – animals that only eat plants.

Native – something that naturally grows or lives in a particular area.

Nectar – a sugary liquid produced by flowers.

Nutrients – substances or ingredients that plants and animals need to live and grow.

Oxygen – an invisible gas in the air that plants produce, and people and animals need to breathe.

Poisonous – something that is very harmful and can cause severe illness or death.

Pollinate – (verb) the process of moving pollen (see below) from one flower to another – often by an insect – so the plant can make new seeds.

Pollen – a dusty powder made by some plants. It is used to produce new seeds.

Pollute – (verb) to make dirty or harmful with waste, chemicals, or other substances.

Sacred – something that is spiritual, and/or worthy of awe and respect.

Sap – a watery substance that comes out of a plant or tree.

Seedling - a young plant, grown from a seed.

Seedpods – pouches or cases produced by some plants to hold their seeds.

Succulents – plants, like cacti, that have fleshy leaves and stems where they store water.

Tannins - bitter-tasting chemicals naturally found in many plant leaves.

Taproot – a tree's thick main root that grows straight down and has smaller roots growing sideways from it.

Index

A

Activities
> Let's Plant a Tree 56–57
> Let's Make a Wildlife Log House 53

Animals 11, 16–17, 20–21, 24–25, 26, 28–29, 30–31, 33, 35, 40, 47, 49, 50–51, 52, 54–55

B

Bark 21, 23, 25, 33, 48–49, 60
Blossom 45, 59, 60
Branches 8–9, 10–11, 13, 22–23, 27, 30, 33, 41
Broadleaf trees 18, 22
Bugs 11, 21, 25, 29, 33, 35, 52–53

C

Cacti 9, 33
Catkins 16, 25
Cones 19, 53
Coniferous trees 19, 22, 41
Crown 8

D

Dangerous trees 27, 43, 48–49
Deciduous trees 18, 22–23
Dormancy 23, 60

E

Evergreen trees 18–19
Extreme environments
> Desert 22–23, 32–33
> Rainforest 26–27, 28–29, 58–59
> Swamp 30–31

F

Flowers 8, 11, 13, 18–19, 22, 24–25, 32, 44–45, 48, 52
Forest 22, 24–25, 40, 42
Fruit 8–9, 11, 13, 16, 18, 22, 26, 29, 36, 43, 47, 48–49
Fungi 24, 34, 40, 60

G

Germination 12, 60
Global warming 55, 60

L

Leaves 8–9, 14, 18–19, 20, 22–23, 27, 29, 32–33, 44, 48, 51, 53, 54

M

Medicine 48–49, 59
Moss 36–37, 53

N

Nutrients 8, 10–11, 20, 23, 29, 33, 34–35, 40, 54, 60
Nuts 17, 25, 27, 58

P

Planting 12–13, 55, 56–57
Pollination 11, 33, 60
Pollution 55, 60

R

Roots 8, 10–11, 12, 23, 27, 30–31, 32–33, 35, 37, 43, 54–55, 56–57

S

Sap 21, 23, 27, 42, 46
Sapling 12, 56–57
Seasons 18–19, 22–23, 56
Seedling 12, 34, 60
Seeds 9, 11, 12, 16–17, 19, 25, 31, 49,
Soil 11, 12, 15, 29, 30–31, 33, 40, 54

T

Tropical trees 26, 29, 48
Trunk 8, 11, 12, 18–19, 27, 33, 36–37, 40–41, 43, 50

W

Water cycle 14–15
Wood 18–19, 37, 40–41, 46–47, 50
Wood wide web 34